Caleb Fleming

The Ingratitude of Infidelity

Proveable from the Humiliation and Exaltation of Jesus Christ

Caleb Fleming

The Ingratitude of Infidelity
Proveable from the Humiliation and Exaltation of Jesus Christ

ISBN/EAN: 9783337148508

Printed in Europe, USA, Canada, Australia, Japan

Cover: Foto ©Lupo / pixelio.de

More available books at **www.hansebooks.com**

Contents

THE

INGRATITUDE OF INFIDELITY:

PROVEABLE FROM THE

HUMILIATION AND EXALTATION

OF

JESUS CHRIST,

BEING

The moſt beneficial Appointments to Mankind, that are within the known Plan of God's moral Government.

ADDRESSED TO

MODERN-DEISTS, JEWS, PAPISTS,

AND

OTHER UNBELIEVERS.

By CALEB FLEMING, D. D.
Paſtor of a Proteſtant Diſſenting Church, who meet at *Pinner's Hall.*

LONDON:
Printed for J. JOHNSON, No. 72, St. *Paul's Church-yard.*
MDCCLXXV.

AN

INTRODUCTORY ADDRESS

TO THE

PUBLIC.

SHOULD it be aſked, what the Author could propoſe, by publiſhing two diſcourſes upon ſuch *trite*, common ſubjects, as thoſe of the humiliation and exaltation of Jeſus Chriſt? his anſwer would be, that the interpretation therein given of them, has afforded him the moſt ſolid ſatisfaction, after about forty years more ſtated inquiry. Hence he has indulged an imagination, that the pleaſing, and delightful view he has been able to take of the Goſpel Inſtitution, in theſe moſt beneficial appointments, may poſſibly lay hold on ſome unbeliever: as well as throw light upon the ſubject, in the opinion of ſome believers. Among thoſe of the latter who affect to monopolize the name of *Orthodox*, he preſumes not upon having many readers. Yet, he hopes for attention from the more liberal and ingenuous inquirers after truth; and for theſe reaſons, *viz.* the doctrinal views he has taken are not ſyſtematical; and, he truſts, they are neither fanciful, nor irrational and groundleſs.

He could moſt earneſtly wiſh that both the *ſceptic*, and the more confirmed modern-deiſt would give them a careful reading; for had he thought infidelity an harmleſs thing,* he would not thus have employed the preſs. And he can aſſure the infidel, that whatever weakneſs he may either find or fancy in the argument, it is the production of benevolence.

Perhaps the PAPIST may take offence at being claſſed with unbelievers; yet, if he could without prejudice calmly conſider, he would aſſuredly know, that his *faith* is not the reſult of a free inquiry; or, of a judgment formed upon the written New Teſtament canon: but it is a merely *implicite credulity* in his Prieſt, and in what his Prieſt calls the church. He ought not, after this, to think himſelf at all inſulted, or ill-uſed by being put into the company of unbelievers. Nay, inaſmuch as he openly rejects

* *Ali*, the ſon-in-law of Mahomet, could ſay, "Infidelity is the cauſe of the removal of God's bleſſing." *Oakley's* Hiſtory of the Saracens, V. ii. p. 338. The Son of God has ſaid, "he that believeth not, ſhall be condemned." Mark xvi. 16.

the

the very firſt or fundamental principles of the chriſtian-religion, *viz.* the acknowledgment of but one God the Father; and of but one mediator between God and man, the man Chriſt Jeſus; he thereby cuts himſelf off from all claim to the character of Chriſtian. In fact, a *papiſt*, as ſuch, has no religion; ſince he has neither eyes nor ears of his own; for he ſacrificeth his reaſon and underſtanding at the altar of *myſtery*; and blindly ſubjugates conſcience to prieſtly dominion. We may moreover, affirm, that no man ever did or ever could become in principle a *Papiſt*, who underſtood the genuine deſign of Chriſt's humiliation and exaltation.*—Where *ignorance is the mother of devotion*, there the homage is only a fit offering to blind, deaf, and dumb idols.

Did the JEW but once make himſelf acquainted with the New Teſtament doctrine of theſe divine appointments, he would ſoon quit his infidelity; and gladly put himſelf under the guidance and government of that ſame Jeſus of Nazareth, who was born a *Jew*; and whom his own nation crucified; but whom God raiſed from the dead and exalted to ſovereignty; and who is the moſt amiable and friendly character in the known

* N. B. Upon a ſuppoſition that the late Pope was poiſoned by the Jeſuits, what muſt be thought of that ſuperſtition?

king-

kingdom of God.—At the ſame time, we are conſtrained to own, that the doctrine of theſe great facts has been, and yet is thickly covered with fanciful opinion and extravagant meaning, ſo as to cheriſh and confirm the prejudices both of Jew and Pagan. Theſe extravagancies, did certainly give riſe to the *Mahometan Impoſture.* Neverthelefs, wherever the doctrine is ſeen and underſtood in its rational, truly great and divine meaning, there its beneficial teachings do powerfully excite the higheſt admiration, thankſgiving, and praiſe.

Such we know is the vaſt importance of our Lord's humiliation and exaltation, as that they have principally engaged the attention of Apoſtles whilſt writing their epiſtles; for theſe facts are what give the genius, ſpirit, and peculiar complexion of thoſe ſacred writings.

As to whatever diſagreement may be found in the Author's conceptions, with thoſe of any of his fellow-chriſtians, he makes no apology; for he owns no human ſtandard either of his faith, hope, or worſhip. Conſcious he is of holding no opinion or principle injurious to any part of the human family. But penetrated with an idea of the alarming ſuperſtructure of ſuperſtition, idolatry and abſurdity, built and building upon the humiliation

miliation and exaltation of Jeſus Chriſt; i. e. being affected painfully with "the "gold, ſilver, precious ſtones, wood, hay, "and ſtubble; that work of man which "ſhall be burnt up, when the fire ſhall try "every man's work of what ſort it is!" he has made this remonſtrance.

Perſuaded he is alſo, that if there be any true religion in the world attended with full evidence, it muſt be that of the chriſtian. Not indeed as it appears in any civil church eſtabliſhment;* nor, in any ſect or party of profeſſors, under the name of *Luther*, *Calvin*, *Arminius*, *Socinus*, *Pelagius*, or others; but as found in the New Teſtament written Code. Neither is it with him probable, that any one profeſſing Chriſtian ſhould be able to form a juſt idea of that religion, who does not derive his knowledge from an unprejudiced, careful, and honeſt examination of that ſacred canon. The *Berean* inquiring ſpirit is the moſt noble: and the idle uninquiring one is the moſt debaſing. In all ſecular purſuits and claims, men demand much better ſecurity—an implicite faith will not ſatisfy them in little things; though it does in great things.

* "*Religion* may be evaporated with little or no da-"mage to the eſtabliſhment." See the CONFESSIONAL, 3d Edit. p. viii.

Finally,

Finally, the Author pretends not to have done more, in these discourses, than to have stated the doctrinal teachings of our Lord's *humiliation* and *exaltation* in a light, which to him appears to be most rational and beneficially instructive; manifesting a *design* full of divinely wise and fatherly goodness! a design, which has the most salutary aspect on a world of creatures made rational, intelligent, and accountable; probationers for a world of recompence. Appointments they therefore are, altogether worthy of that infinite spirit, who is supremely adorable in the whole of the Gospel-discoveries made both of his truth and grace; and which must consequently fix the charge of *ingratitude* upon the unbeliever, who may consult the evidence.

Whatever imperfections may be found in the method, style, language, or sentiment; these discourses speak the genuine conceptions of a man who must, according to the course of nature, soon have a personal interview with that same divine personage, whom the one God the Father has constituted the one Lord both over the dead and over the living.—

Hoxton-Square,
Jan. 20. 1775.

ON THE

HUMILIATION

OF

JESUS CHRIST.

ST. John, who perfectly well underſtood the nature and evidence of the Chriſtian Inſtitution, ſays, "Hereby perceive we the love "*of God*, becauſe he laid down his life for us; "and we ought to lay down our lives for the "brethren." See his firſt epiſtle, third chapter and ſixteenth verſe.—

There is not any thing which more diſtinguiſheth the Goſpel-religion from all others, than the divine benevolence which it breathes towards mankind; and the apt tendency which its docrines have, to inſpire all ſincere profeſſors with that ſame divine ſpirit. It has all the characteriſtic lines and features of an heavenly complexion; for this reaſon it claims a ſuperlative excellence; and has this peculiar glory, that it is the *laſt*, and therefore muſt be the moſt perfect revelation which ſhall ever be made of the truth and grace of God, in this probationary ſtate of man. No other diſcoveries can he expect to be made of the divine mind, until the future openings of the hea-

 venly

venly scenes. Which openings, will rather be a revelation of the *final consequences* of virtue and piety, and of their contraries, by the judicial determination of the man Christ Jesus, whom God has appointed to judge the world in righteousness. Of the certainty of which, he has given ground of credit to all men, in that he has raised him from the dead.

It is an humiliating view which we take of the depravity of the professing Christian world, *viz.* that the great design of the death of Christ, seems to be but very little understood. The which ungrateful truth, affords a powerful reason why it should be yet farther considered, and held up to the public eye, in some more rational point of view. Attend we then to this apostolical declaration. And let us,

I. Enquire how it is we may perceive that the love of God is made manifest, because, or by reason of Jesus Christ laying down his life for us. And

II. What is the extensive spirit of benevolence, which it lays every Christian under to the brethren.

Here it should be observed, that the word God, is scarce found in any of the Greek copies, and is not in the Syriac, as critics have remarked. But it runs thus, *hereby perceive we the* LOVE; because, &c. The love is then emphatical. Now a careful reader of this Epistle will find, that the love of God is the burden of its address. And it is the *manner* of love which the

the Father hath beſtowed upon us, in calling us his ſons, which gives the ſpirit of the foregoing context. Perſonal moral righteouſneſs, is what conſtitutes the filiation. And for the purpoſe of promoting this, "the Son of God was mani-"feſted, that he might deſtroy the works of the "devil." Conſequently, the love here mentioned in my text, muſt reſpect the divine meaſures of promoting man's righteouſneſs, and diſcountenancing his unrighteouſneſs.

Certain it is, that the love here mentioned, has not to do with things of a ſecular and civil nature; but it is a love which St. *John* is illuſtrating, as it has for its object, the ſuperlative good of man. No one can acquaint himſelf well with the New Teſtament canon, but muſt be perſuaded, that its ſalutary *grace*, favour, or love, neither is, nor can be expreſſed by the ſenſitive, the material, periſhing good; foraſmuch as its profeſſed deſign is, to take off the eye of the chriſtian from the things that are viſible and earthly; and to fix his firſt deſire upon things inviſible and heavenly. It would perſuade to a mortifiedneſs to the world, and to all its treaſures; in other words, it would implant a ſettled averſion in him to its luſtings, evil-maxims and manners.

Indeed the love which God has for us, is a fatherly concern for our becoming regular, virtuous, and amiable in the whole of our morals; as what will render us peaceful, comfortable, and happy in every mode and ſituation of our exiſtence.

We cannot possibly mistake in this idea which we form of divine love; since it is expressive of the most adorable benevolence; which will thus be manifest, *viz.* if we form any rational conception of his *wisdom* and *goodness* who gave us being; we must be persuaded, he could not be unconcerned about or unmindful of our attaining to those ends, which essential love did propose by giving us existence:—But those ends, could be nothing less than our moral rectitude; the *basis* of all real and permanent felicity. We have no other way of either perceiving or experiencing the *love* here mentioned, which gives the significance and beneficial importance of all Gospel address.—

St. *John* placeth before us, a special and indisputable instance of this love, in that he whom God had manifested to destroy the works of the devil, has *laid down his life for us.* We may then be absolutely certain, that *he* who thus laid down his life, could not be God: He could not, forasmuch as the Greek word (Ψυχη) rendered *life*, signifies what breathes and respires; and therefore is by no means applicable to God: it is too low, gross, and creaturely an idea; it supposes something organized, which may be parted-with, given up, resigned, and even extinguished. A very debased and dishonourable apprehension of the first cause, and creator of all; since no liableness to a painful passiveness can be applicable to an infinte, unchangeable, eternal spirit: the supposition of any possible abatement of his enlivening influences and impressions would sicken all nature, and enfeeble the whole creation; the thought

thought of any poſſible change in him would be horrible! and inſupportably ſhocking!

Theſe are not to be reckoned idle, impertinent, or needleſs remarks, when we have ſuch numbers around us ſo depraved, by their wild conceptions and aſtoniſhing credulity, as to aſcribe thoſe abſolute incommunicable perfections to a man who laid down his life; which aſcriptions, would conclude him unoriginated and independent; for how common is it for men to ſpeak of Jeſus Chriſt, *as God equal with the Father in power and glory*, as well as alſo *of the ſame ſubſtance?* The daring impiety ſtares in ones face, as we walk the ſtreets of this great city: the Popiſh hand-writing upon the walls, is, JESUS CHRIST IS THE ETERNAL GOD, JEHOVAH! whereas his laying down his life, determines him to be truly and properly man. And that he would do this, he himſelf beforehand declared to his diſciples more than once.* We cannot therefore miſtake in applying the perſon whom St. *John* ſpeaks of in the text, to the *man Chriſt Jeſus*; that good ſhepherd, who did not only lay down his life for the ſheep, but who received *a commandment from the Father*, which rendered it ſo highly fit and proper he ſhould ſo do: For, in truth, he had not made any forfeiture of life: neither did he lie expoſed to the common ſentence of mortality. If therefore his life was taken away, it muſt be by his own conſent, and in an obedient conformity to the plan of his divine miſſion; of which he had been previouſly informed by the Father.

* *Joh.* x. 15, 17, 18. And Chap. xv. 13.

The great end for which he laid down his life, was, to demonstrate the *love of God* to mankind, in that he laid it down FOR US. And hence it is that he says, "therefore does my Father "love me, because I lay down my life for the sheep."

The great inquiry will now be, in what respects he did truly die FOR US; i. e. for our benefit?—

But here we should premise a few things—Jesus Christ, did not give his murderers the least ground of accusation, either of impiety, or crime: there was not so much as any guile found in his lips; and he even held up beforehand to their eye, the aggravated crime they would commit, the enormous guilt they would contract, by their ungrateful and cruel treatment of him. Nay, he even led them to pass that sentence of condemnation upon themselves.*

Neither did he die in our room and stead: this was impossible; because he was no sinner: nor could he sustain either the guilt or the punishment of sin. So that in the eye of truth and of God, he could neither have our iniquities imputed to him, nor sustain the demerit of them: For, "though he died the just by the hands of "the unjust;" yet, he could not die in their room and stead: but it was by *wicked* hands he was crucified and slain. The very Roman Governour who passed the sentence of death upon him, declared his innocence before all the peo-

* Matt. xxi. 33 to 40.

ple; and he never once owned, that he could be chargeable with, or accountable for others crimes.—

Again, his laying down his life for us, does not imply in it an atoning, placating ſacrifice; calculated to appeaſe and reconcile the holy God; or to make him more propitious to a world of ſinful creatures: But it was to demonſtrate, that Deity, is, in his own nature, and in all his meaſures with mankind, PROPITIOUS. Hence it was, he appointed that Jeſus Chriſt ſhould lay down his life, in order to reconcile ſinners to himſelf; or, that he ſhould thus die, "the juſt by the "hands of the unjuſt, that he might *bring us to* "*God*." His death was truly a PROPITIATORY, which more than anſwered to the mercy-ſeat, with which the Jews had been favoured: foraſmuch as a demonſtration is thereby given, that a righteous God does not impute ſin to the penitent; ſince *repentance and remiſſion of ſins* was the expreſs divine meſſage to his murderers—Apoſtles were to begin to proclaim this general pardon *firſt* at Jeruſalem. Not any conceiveable event could have given ſuch demonſtration of the merciful nature of God; thus pure, unmerited, unpurchaſed divine love to a ſinful world, is rendered illuſtrious, in the appointment of Chriſt's death. A method of making the manifeſtation, quite out of the reach of any created, derived goodneſs either to have deſigned, or contrived; and which idea, I apprehend St. Paul had, when he calls the doctrine of the croſs, (in the eye of men) the *fooliſhneſs* of God, and the *weakneſs* of God.—And yet, how very wonderful is the *apparatus* of prophecy running through all the ages of the world, for ſo many thousand years! and abundantly confirmed by miracle.—

But here observe, we are not to stop short in the event of Christ's death; for he himself has said, "therefore does my Father love me, because "I lay down my life, *that I might take it up* "*again.*" We are, accordingly, to carry our views onward to his ascension to the right hand of power; and to those high offices which he sustains as the one Lord. We thus take a view of *the joy that had been set before him:* the recompence of reward which was to be bestowed on him by the Father; "who, in order to the bringing "of many sons to glory, thus made the captain of their salvation perfect through sufferings." So far therefore is the death of Christ from being the measure of *reconciling God to men*, that the most express doctrine of the cross, is, *to reconcile men to God*, and an Apostle thus argues, "we being reconciled unto God by the death of "his son, much more shall we be saved by his "life."—

Artful priests, and deluded systematical professors are wont to lay the emphasis of man's salvation, *wholly* upon the death of Christ; whereas, there could have been no meaning, no efficacy at all in his death, had he not risen again. So says St. *Paul*, "if Christ be not raised, your faith is "vain, you are yet in your sins."* A full proof that his death was not the purchase of remission, or the term of man's justification in the sight of

* 1 Cor. xv. 17.

God;

God; "for though he was delivered for our offences, or, to expose the malignity of sin; yet "he was raised again for our justification;" for by this means it is, that our hopes in the mercy of God unto *eternal life*, are justified.* There could not then be any atoning virtue in his death, when applied to God; but it was to give us an abhorrence of sin; and to cure us of all faulty dispositions; to purge our consciences from dead works; and to enable us to serve the living God.

Again, his obedience to the death, cannot be a compensation, or make the least satisfaction for our want of obedience: i. e. it cannot, by any means, be imputed to us, or reckoned as our obedience, however strong our faith is in his having been perfectly conformable to the divine will, throughout his very painful endurance.

The idea is absurd and full of extravagance, and a very perverse application of the design of his death. In truth, for us to suppose, that either the obedience or the disobedience of another can be reckoned ours, is to confound all ideas of truth and right: it is to rob the holy God of the glory of his perfections; and to deny there is any equity in his ways, or any righteousness in his dealings with man: he would no longer be an object of our trust, hope, or confidence; neither should we be able to pay the least regard to his moral government. The romantic idea of a *transfer* either of righteousness or of sin, is extremely reproachful to the christian profession: not any

* Rom. iv. 25.

idea or notion being more dishonourable to the Supreme Governor.

On the other hand, the love of God, rightly understood, in the appointment of the death of Christ, has *wisdom* and *goodness* in it which demands our admiration, thanksgiving and praise! inasmuch as it has shewn the *inefficacy* of all symbolical bloody sacrifice, by having far more expressively exposed the *evil* of sin, or of that worldliness which had covered the earth with ignorance, superstition, idolatry and vice. The malignity of which worldliness flagrantly appeared, in mens putting to death God's well-beloved Son, by whom he had revealed all his truth and all his grace. Even the most illustrious displays of omnipotent goodness, throughout his ministrations, had not been sufficient to prevent such an unexampled outrage of impiety and crime.

In consequence of this depraved state of the world, the PARACLETE, or *promise of the Father*, was to convince the world of sin; because they had not believed on him who had had the most complete credentials to a divine character and mission:—and to convince also of the unspeakable advantage *of righteousness*; since, by virtue of his obedience he is gone to the Father; and is by him placed at the right hand of power;—and also to convince *of judgement:* because the prince of this world is judged; which I should read convince of *condemnation*; because a worldly spirit is by him condemned; which worldly spirit, is called the prince of this world:* Here is a fulness of

* John xiv. 30.

force, energy, and efficacy in the evidence. *Moreover*, as his death was the pre-requisite to his after-appointments, so the openings of a future state, under the administration of this crucified man, do abundantly shew, the salutary sense in which he laid down his life for us; for so it is that all the precious promises are in him *yea*, and in him *amen*, to the praise and glory of God the Father; and we thus perceive the emphatical love there was in his laying down his life for us.

We are in the *second* place, to take some notice of that extensive benevolence which it lays every christian under to the brethren: the text says, "and we ought to lay down our lives for the "brethren."—It may be asked, who are the *brethren?* I should answer, the *christians.*—Indeed I find this description given of *Christianity* in a late publication, *viz.*—"The view which christ"ianity always gives of *mankind* is the natural "one, a community of brethren, the free and "equal subjects of a divine government, the heirs "of immortality, and the sons of God."—Which I should take to be a much more proper description of the Christian-church, than of mankind in general; as its divine touches and lineaments *sons of God*, *heirs of immortality*, are what give a *peculiar* lustre and excellence to the last dispensation of the truth and grace of God. Besides, the compellation, *brethren*, in the New Testament writings, is usually characteristic of christians. In my text it must have this precise meaning, and does aptly distinguish them from the unbelieving world. So it is St. *Peter* would be understood when he says, *honour all men, love the*

the brotherhood;—agreeably to which the bleſſed Jeſus is wont to ſpeak of believers in him, as a *little flock*; a diſtinct community from the reſt of mankind; and he prays for them, as men *hated* by the world.

What are we now to underſtand, by *laying down our lives for the brethren?*—at the very firſt view it ſeems plainly to import, the utmoſt ſtretch of human benevolence; anſwerable to that obſervation of our Lord's, " greater love hath no " man than this, that a man lay down his life " for his friends."—Now if the New Teſtament doctrine of Chriſt's death be carefully examined, it will be found, that its beneficial or ſalutary effect is always ſpecified under ſome moral influence and beneficial impreſſion which it makes upon the human mind. Some good diſpoſition which it is calculated to promote. And to the chriſtian it is the great examplar or pattern of the moſt perfect human benevolence; but if whilſt mankind univerſally lay in a ſtate of enmity to *truth* and *goodneſs*, God's meſſenger, and beloved ſon Jeſus Chriſt, bore teſtimony to their infinite importance, by laying down his life in their cauſe, and for their ſupport; we thereby have a demonſtration given, that the rectitude of the human mind, its qualification for happineſs does wholly conſiſt in an unreſerved obedience to the will of God; or in a ſtedfaſt conformity to that will, under the ſevereſt trials of humanity. This being the caſe, the Chriſtian, in imitation of his Lord, ought to be willing and ready to lay down his life for the brethren, whenever the cauſe of Goſpel truth requires ſuch teſtimony; i. e. he is to ſhew a like devotedneſs to the divine will, and a like

like benevolence towards the children of truth and goodneſs.

It aſſuredly cannot intend, we ſhould draw the ſword, or expoſe our lives in an hoſtile manner for the defence of the *brethren*; it cannot: for the religion of Jeſus utterly diſowns and condemns any unfriendly, inimical, or bloody meaſures in its propagation, or defence. It abhors both the *Mahometan*, and the *Popiſh* ſpirit, and in its cauſe, will not permit the uſe of any offenſive weapon whatſoever. It puts none to pain, torture, or death. Nor does it allow of any the leaſt malevolence towards the unbeliever. It requires a readineſs to lay down our lives in teſtimony of the high eſteem and veneration we have of our holy religion, whenever the hand of perſecution makes the demand upon us; or when, in the language of an ingenious pen, "we have "nothing left us to do, but to remonſtrate and "ſuffer."*

This devotedneſs to the cauſe of truth, is not only to operate in an age of perſecution, but will upon all occaſions whatſoever which try the patience, meekneſs, and fortitude of the chriſtian. His temper and behaviour will uniformly ſhew, he has ſuch ideas of God's love to the world, made manifeſt in his Son's laying down his life for us, as habitually diſpoſe him to devote all his powers to the ſervice, and in the cauſe of truth and virtue; an imitation of his Lord, that is moſt beneficial to the brethren. Herein the ſame ſpirit of benevolence operates in the

* A friend in North Britain.

chriſtian

christian which did operate in him "who gave "himself for us, that he might deliver us from "the evil of this present world;" and conspicuously place before us the most joyous prospects of the final recompence; an assurance being thereby given of *eternal life* to all, who by a patient continuance in well-doing, do seek glory, honour, and immortality! In a word, the moral obligation, here mentioned by St. *John*, arising from the death of Christ, intends, our being possessed of and animated by that same spirit of benevolence, which always consults the reputation and honour of our holy religion; and renders it amiable in the eyes of all, who see our conversation to be thus exemplary towards our brethren.

If the apostolic observation has been rightly understood, several useful instructions will be deducible therefrom.—Such as,

I. The most interesting and engaging capital truth, held up to us in the death of Christ, is, the *love of God to mankind.* His death certainly is the most convincing evidence that can be given of God's good-will to a sinful world; as it proves him placable and propitious to the worst of sinners. "Go, *says the risen Jesus*, preach repent-"ance and remission of sins to all nations; and "begin at Jerusalem, the city of my murder-"ers! Let them and all mankind know, that "God would have none of his human offspring "perish; but would have all of us come to re-"pentance: or, to a knowledge of the truth, "and be saved." This is the express doctrine of Christ's death; therefore there could be no marks of divine displeasure shewn to the blessed Jesus,

in

in the article of his sufferings; there could not possibly be any thing like the least token of God's displeasure to a well beloved Son, who was expressing the highest act of obedience and resignation to the will of his Father, in thus laying down his life for us.

They therefore must have very injustifiable notions of the *Supreme*, who imagine, he poured out his wrath upon his obedient beloved Son, in whom he was always well pleased. On the contrary, he saw, he approved, he delighted in the singularly instructive, and most compleat examplar of obedience. Nay, our blessed Lord himself had the consciousness that his whole behaviour under the severest trials of humanity, was not only approved of, but would be abundantly rewarded by his Father: he knew he had not forsaken him; though the chief priests and people looked upon him and reviled him as if he had: *They did esteem him stricken, smitten of God, forsaken.*

Again, notwithstanding the atrocious wickedness of his murderers, who had accumulated a most aggravated guilt, deserving of the hottest vengeance; yet so far from pouring down his wrath upon this ungrateful provoking people, the merciful, long suffering God, vouchsafed to the truly penitent murderer, not only pardon, but the promise of eternal life; for though at the crucifixion, the holy God gave them awful and alarming evidence of this matchless impiety, by the earth's trembling, the rocks rending, the sun's withdrawing his rays! yet the offended Majesty proceeded not to swallow up that wicked city, which had perpetrated the most daring and provoking

voking insults to the *light of the world!* that great revealer of divine truth and grace.

As to those *Jews* who remained impenitent, and retained an hatred of truth, these, having filled up the measure of their iniquity, either fell a sacrifice to the Roman vengeance; or else became vagabonds, scattered over the face of the earth: and to this day, are but wanderers, vainly expecting that promised deliverer, whom their nation had rejected and crucified.

One might now ask, who is it that cannot perceive the *love of God* made illustrious in this great event? who can contemplate the death of Christ, and not discover it to be the most powerful persuasive display ever made of God's love to mankind? for by means of that finished act of obedience to the divine will, the malignity of worldliness is exposed in all its flagrant enormity! Sin could not have appeared so exceedingly sinful, nor a love of truth so divinely powerful a principle, had not Jesus Christ given such demonstration of it, by *laying down his life for us.*

II. No man is able to form a right judgment of the *reason* and *end* of Christ's death, who does not consider it in an inseparable connexion with its consequences; or, unless he takes into his view, those *effects* which are ascribed to its *causality*; for an apostle says, that "because he humbled himself, and became obedient unto death, "even the death of the cross; therefore God did "highly exalt him, giving him a name above "every name:" For which reason we are to comprehend along with his death, its consequences, as they did affect himself; a firm trust and confidence in which, was what enabled our Lord thus to glorify his Father, who delighted to exalt him; and also because of the beneficial effects which his death has upon mankind; in that the adorable God in his infinite wisdom and goodness, has been pleased to exemplify in him, the plan of his benevolence and abundant mercy towards mankind. We can also at the same time, enjoy the distinguished honour he has been pleased to confer on one of our own species; by constituting him the prime minister of his providence, and the instrument used by him of raising the dead, and judging the world.

Now, admitting these views of Christ's death to be not only real, but divinely *wise* and *good*, every way beneficial to mankind, we are naturally led to solace ourselves in this event, and make it the subject-matter of our rejoicing before God. St. *Paul* did so, who said, "he determined to "know nothing * save Jesus Christ, and him "crucified:" and *again*, "he would glory in the "cross of Christ, by which the world was cruci-"fied unto him, and he unto the world."—Not to do this, must be disingenuous and ungrateful.

III. Since the Christian is capable of imitating his Lord, or resembling him even in his death, by laying down his own life for the brethren; it is evident, that what is so currently called the *orthodox* opinion of the death of Christ, cannot be just, nor tenable. No one, I pre-

* i. e. Nothing so much as Jesus Christ, &c.

sume, will dare to affirm, that the christian's laying down his life for the brethren, can operate like a *price* paid to divine justice, or as a compensation; and to satisfy the demands of a violated law, in behalf of the brethren: this would be too open an absurdity; too bold an extravagance:—and yet, how many are there who will have it, that the blood of Christ has this very appeasing effect? Indeed, the *doctrine of satisfaction* is amazingly prevalent; and sadly depraves the sentiments of men, called christians; for it leads to a false refuge and dependence, inasmuch as thereby men are pleading a claim, and fixing a reliance upon the merits of Christ's blood for their justification and acceptance with God, to which they can have no manner of right. And moreover, they thus exclude the very idea of God's pardoning mercies being unmerited and free: forasmuch as if he has received a *price*, or a satisfaction has been made on account of the sinner's crime and guilt, in the nature of a compensation, or a purchase of his pardon, there can be no favour or mercy in the justification. The pardoned sinner, so far from being indebted to the love of God, is solely beholden to the benevolence of Jesus Christ.

These apprehensions are extremely dishonourable and disingenuous to the love of God! They are a shameful perversion of the design of Christ's laying down his life for us. But verily, there is a much more rational, just, and satisfactory sense to be given of that singularly great event, *viz.* that of its moral effect, inspiring with the spirit of divine benevolence, which is seen in the christian's being thereby led to an *imitation* of his Lord, in laying down his life for the brethren.

IV. Methinks, no one can read the New Testament with an honest and unprejudiced mind, without being convinced, that Jesus Christ did enjoin upon all his disciples and followers, a thankful celebration of the memorials of his death. But this being the truth of the case, it must appear to be very surprising, that so very few professors do reckon themselves under that obligation. It cannot but be matter of painful concern to a benevolent mind, that one of the very plainest and most express of our Lord's injunctions or institutions, in the celebration of which he has the fullest demonstration that was ever given of the *love of God*, should be the least understood and observed among professing christians. A lively writer, in some sermons lately published, has spoken thus nervously upon this subject—he says, "he should be glad there was "no distinction in his society between worshippers and communicants; for we must have "very extraordinary charity to suppose a man a "real disciple of Christ, at the same time that he "neglects a request, a desire of his master, given "under circumstances that must sensibly affect his "heart, and solely addressed to his humanity and "gratitude."—*He adds*, "in the apostolic age, "for a man to have pretended to be a christian, "and not attend the memorial rite, would have "been as absurd, as if one should pretend to religious character, whose conduct was prophane "and immoral."* So far my Author.

* David Williams's Sermons, Vol. 1. p. 142. and 180.

Some learned and good men have, I apprehend, carried the obligation to an extreme by pleading for *Infant-Communion*; which surely can have no tendency to recommend the celebration of the memorial rite; since there is no ability either of self-examination, or any capacity of discovering the moral intention. ‡ Yet, as soon as our youth, of either sex, are capable of contemplating the love of God, as displayed in our Lord's laying down his life for us, or can see that it condemns all worldly lustings, they ought to celebrate the memorial rite. That learned and amiable confessor, Mr. T. EMLYN, has said, "so "long as this memorial was kept up, so long "the christian religion could never be defaced; "and this being handed down from one age to "another, became a standing evidence of the "matter

‡ It differs greatly from Baptism, which when applied either to infants or grown persons, only initiates into a kingdom, wherein Jesus Christ presides as the one Lord; and entitles to the privileges and immunities of that kingdom. Thus the first converts and their housholds were distinguished from the families of unbelievers, both among Jews and Gentiles; and thus the infant-offspring of Christians are put under the protection and government of that one Lord, and are to be educated in the nurture and admonition of his teachings. Whereas, in the celebration of the Eucharist, there must be a distinguishing mind in the communicant; he is to *discern the Lord's body, having examined himself*, and seen the reason and use of this memorial rite. I presume no unprejudiced man, who reads St. *Paul's* account of this Institution, the qualification of the communicant, the abusive perversions of it among the Corinthians,* would once be led to suppose any infants were communicated.

And should we be of opinion, that the *Eucharist* did succeed and supersede the passover, it does not appear that infants had ever eat of that memorial lamb: for we have no account of the child Jesus being taken to that festival at Jerusalem till

* 1 Cor. xi. 20. end.

he

"matter of fact on which christianity is found-"ed."† What that matter of fact was, See *Tit.* ii. 14. *Gal.* i. 4. *John* xvii. 14, 15. and many other places.

V. From the powerful influence which *a love of truth* actually had within the breast of the blessed Jesus, we can conclude with confidence the *superiority* over all temptation which it will give to every one so animated: as is to be seen in the astonishing serenity and calmness preserved in our Lord, under a series of unexampled provocations! Indeed the greatness of his behaviour under the insults of his enemies, and the tortures of a crucifixion,‡ is no other way to be accounted for, but from his love of truth

he was twelve years of age; which was agreeable to the Jewish custom: but before that time he is not said to have been with his parents, though they went up every year. *Luk.* ii. 41, 42.

The argument of the learned PIERCE adopted by the very celebrated ~~Dr.~~ PRIESTLEY, as taken from a custom that obtained in an early age of the Church, has no binding authority; for many extravagancies were introduced by both Jewish and Pagan converts. No traces of infant communion are to be found in the New Testament canon; but its whole testimony is against the practice. Had it been intended for infants, would not our Lord, or his apostles have informed us? one thing I see in the disgustful idea of Infant Communion, which it is to be supposed these great men would condemn, *viz.* it would countenance the giving of the Eucharist to the dying, or *in articulo mortis*; since, with them, it does not require any knowledge of its intention in the receiver. And the Quaker as well as others might well look upon it, as a childish and unmeaning ritual. *Do this in remembrance of me:* cannot be an injunction upon infants.

† Emlyn's *Tracts*, Vol. iii. p. 240.

‡ Consult Dr LARDNER's excellent Sermon, *on the greatness of Jesus in his last suffering.*

and God; which was what filled him with ſo much concern to recover and ſave a loſt world, deluged in ignorance, ſuperſtition, idolatry and vice.

After all, it is extremely difficult to perſuade men of the infinite importance of an unreſerved devotedneſs to the will of God; and yet, no mathematical demonſtration can be more clear and convincing: but the difficulty ariſes from an averſion to religious inquiries, and to the labors of virtue. A faulty education, rooted prejudice, bad example, faſhionable evil-maxims and cuſtoms, do enervate the mind ſo much, as to rob its powers and faculties of their freedom; and reduce them to a ſlaviſh ſubjection to the tyranny of the appetites and paſſions. Ignorance, idolatry, and ſuperſtition have taught men to build upon this ſingular unparallelled act of obedience, a ſuperſtructure, quite full of rank and offenſive abſurdity: and much weakneſs, inconſiſtency and preſumption, have taken place of thoſe genuine effects, *viz.* ſerenity, regularity, fortitude, and firmneſs of mind under the preſſures of mortality; though theſe foundations of exiſtence are found to be ſolid and unſhaken, and the reliſhes of them truly refined, ſatisfying, and refreſhing. They manifeſtly diſown MATERIALISM; and allow it to have no relation at all to the ſpiritual and moral ſyſtem, or to the life-principle of immortality.

It muſt be owned, that the doctrine of Chriſt's death, has been deplorably depraved and corrupted in the popular opinions; inſomuch that the mind of the unbeliever revolts and takes offence at the

the repreſentations which are full of nonſenſe and impenetrable myſtery:—but however keen may be the infidel ſneer, we may be well aſſured of this, *viz.* that the New Teſtament doctrine of the death of Chriſt, as it evinceth the love of God, ſo it ſhews the energy there is in a love of that ſyſtem of truth, which has enough in it, either to *ſink* an unbelieving, or to *ſave* a believing world.—"To God only wiſe, be glory "through Jeſus Chriſt for ever. Amen."

ON THE

EXALTATION

OF

JESUS CHRIST.

Col. i. 15. to the 19th verſe incluſively,—"Who "is the image of the inviſible God, the firſt-"born of every creature: for by him were all "things created that are in heaven, and that are "in earth, viſible and inviſible, whether thrones, "or dominions, or principalities, or powers: "all things were created by him and for him. "And he is before all things, and by him all "conſiſt; and he is the head of the body the "church: who is the beginning, the firſt-born "from the dead; that in all things he might "have the pre-eminence. For it pleaſed *the* "*Father*, that in him ſhould all fulneſs dwell."

THAT celebrated eccleſiaſtical hiſtorian and biblical Critic, the late Reverend Dr. LARDNER, has ſhewn, that "this epiſtle was probably written and ſent to the church at Coloſſe "towards the end of the year of Chriſt 62; "about the ſame time with that written to the "Philippians, and in the ſecond year of St. *Paul's* "impriſonment at Rome. And alſo that it is

"reaſon-

" reaſonable to conclude, this ſame apoſtle had " planted a church there; for St. *Luke* in- " forms us, of his having been twice in Phrygia, " in which were the three capital cities of *Coloſſe*, " *Laodicea*, and *Hierapolis*. See *Acts* xvi. 6. and " *ch.* xviii. 23. He alſo informs us, that the apoſtle " went over all the countries of Galatia and Phrygia " in order, ſtrengthening the brethren, ch. xix. 1. " In both of his journeys it is reaſonable to con- " clude, he would viſit theſe chief cities."*

In this epiſtle, the apoſtle expreſſes great ſolicitude about the chriſtians at Coloſſe, that they would profeſs the chriſtian doctrine in its purity; keeping themſelves free from erroneous conceptions of its truth and grace. And he urges their thankful acknowledgment for the knowledge they had of God; a people who had lately been more generally ignorant and idolatrous Gentiles; he would have them direct their homage " to God the Father, who had made them meet " to be partakers of the inheritance of the Saints " in light; and had delivered them from the " power of darkneſs, and tranſlated them into the " kingdom of his dear Son; in whom they " had redemption through his blood, even the for- " giveneſs of ſins."

He proceeds, in the words of my text, to delineate the delegated dignity and pre-eminence of Jeſus Chriſt. A reaſon of which was evidently this,—they had, in their Gentiliſm, been accuſtomed to worſhip *Gods many, and Lords many:*

* See his ſupplement, Vol. ii. and the chapter on this Epiſtle.

but

but now, as chriſtians they are to acknowledge only one God, and one Lord; in which unity of idea, they would find themſelves free from all confuſion in their religious worſhip.—

This premiſed,—in diſcourſing upon this figurative deſcription here given of that dignity which the great God has conferred on the man Chriſt Jeſus; I would *Firſt*, attempt the genuine ſenſe and meaning of the deſcription. *Secondly*, enumerate ſome of its moſt highly beneficial inſtructions to mankind.

Much obſcurity, I apprehend, has been thrown upon this account of our Lord's exaltation. In attempting the ſenſe of ſo very ſublime a deſcription, a careful view ſhall be taken of it, in the order in which it lies before us.—

And the firſt thing which our apoſtle ſays of Jeſus Chriſt, is, *that he is the image of the inviſible God.*—Now an *image* may be either an artificial repreſentation, or viſible likeneſs taken by the pencil, chiſel, &c. of a viſible material object: Yea, it may be whatever has an apt tendency to raiſe in us juſt ideas and conceptions of what is inviſible. For *example*, the informing ſpirit and power of language, either by the lip or by letters, will give us the image of one anothers inward thoughts, tempers, diſpoſitions, deſigns, or of the mental complexion; as will alſo in ſome degree, be diſcovered by the eye, the air and mien, and outward geſture of a man.

That

That the apoftle could not by the word, *image*, intend an artificial, figured, corporeal, vifible reprefentation and form of that which has no figure or bodily-form, is felf-evident; forafmuch as by reafon of the Archetype of the image having no form nor figure, and being abfolutely invifible; becaufe without limit or boundary of prefence; it is impoffible that the vifible figured, circumfcribed, organized man Jefus Chrift, fhould in that fenfe be the image of God. There can be no fimilitude poffibly taken of what is infinite and immenfe; no adequate, no competent idea can be formed, no comprehenfive metaphyfical idea of an infinite, uncaufed Being. But in the other fenfe of an *image*, underftood as what has an apt tendency to raife in us an idea or conception of what is abfolutely invifible, or of what is the internal purpofe, the will, defire or defign of another intelligent being, our Jefus may be juftly ftiled, the *image of the invifible God*; inafmuch as he has been enabled fully to reveal to us what is the determinate, immutable mind and will of the invifible God.—In which fenfe, he is fo perfect an image of him, as to fay, "he that "hath feen me, hath feen the Father;—and I "and the Father are one;"—which can only be underftood of that faithful and complete revelation which he has made of the will of God, confidered both as Governor and Father; for God's truth and grace he has made plainly intelligible to man. Nay, fo far as we ourfelves are attempered and formed by that manifeftation which he has made of the mind and will of God; fo far we are alfo made in the image of the invifible God,—fo fays St. Paul, ch. iii. 10. of this epiftle—"putting on the new man, we are "renewed

" renewed in righteouſneſs, after the image of him " who created us."—I might add, that *Adam*, the firſt parent of mankind, was created in the image of God; becauſe capable of knowing and doing his will, and becauſe he had a dominion aſſigned him over the lower creation.

Whereby we are led to another view, in which the man Chriſt Jeſus may be ſaid to be the image of the inviſible God; and that is, his being appointed to a ſupreme dominion; *the firſt-born of every creature.*

The Greek word (πρωτοτοκος) rendered *firſt-born*, cannot mean the *firſt* in order of time, but in office, rank, and dignity; he had a name given him *above* every name; not *before* every name. The firſt born imports, *excellence*; and has reſpect to a *new*, and not to the *old* creation: *viz.* the Goſpel-kingdom, the laſt and finiſhed diſpenſation of God's truth and grace And hence *all things that are in heaven, and that are in earth, viſible and inviſible, whether thrones, or dominions, or principalities, or powers, are ſaid to be* CREATED *by him and for him.*—

Here it ſhould be carefully obſerved, that the word rendered, *create*, does not by any means ſignify, that they were brought into exiſtence by him; but as the great LOCKE well remarked, St. Paul is wont to ſpeak of the Goſpel-diſpenſation, as a *new creation*; and of the converts to chriſtianity as *new creatures.* So that he uſeth the word (κτισις) which literally ſignifies a proper creation; or, a bringing into exiſtence that which was not; but muſt here have a figua figurative, or a metaphorical meaning, and import, a *change of condition:* * for the same apostle, when speaking of the mystery which from the beginning had been hid in God, who *created* all things by Jesus Christ; must undoubtedly have a reference to the all things in this *new* and heavenly kingdom.—To the same purpose, it is observed "of the Hebrew word *Bara*, which "signifies in the literal sense to create, whenever "applied to God's bringing into existence what "had not been before:" yet, even that same word is applied in a very figurative sense in the Hebrew scriptures, as in Numb. xvi. 30. to extraordinary divine operations, in which there is no production of any *new* being; but it is used for the earth's being made to swallow up *Korah* and his company; and for the wonderful scenery, Exod. xxiv. 10. And for the moral renewal of the human heart, "*create* in me a clean heart, "O God," Psal. li. 10. and for the divine influences in his moral kingdom; "I form "the light, and create darkness, I make peace "and create evil." † And *once more*, it is used for the putting a nation into a new and more happy condition, Isa. xliii. 1. and 15. Which last use of the term, will throw much light upon the *creation* spoken of in the text: all things in heaven and in earth, visible and invisible, having Jesus Christ placed at their head, are, for that very reason, said to be created by him and for him. It is therefore with propriety said,

* See his notes on Eph. iii. 9.

† See Dr. D. Jenning's introduction to the Globes, p. 162. and Dr. Taylor's Hebrew Concordance, No. 224. Isa. xlv. 7.

And he is before all things, and by him all things CONSIST. So that there is no want of regularity, order, and harmony throughout the plan of his adminiſtration in God's kingdom. With which agree the accounts given of him in the firſt chapter of the epiſtle to the Hebrews, where the Angels are commanded to obey his orders, and ſo to worſhip him. And can we now wonder, that an apoſtle who was a Jew, and converſant with the Hebrew ſcriptures ſhould uſe the word *create*, in a figurative ſenſe, when ſpeaking of our Lord's exaltation? we cannot, when we have found that the prophets of old had ſo uſed the word *create*; and eſpecially when we conſider that metaphor is common in all languages. To proceed,

And he is the head of the body, the church.

In the epiſtle to the Epheſians, this apoſtle ſays, "God has placed Jeſus Chriſt far above "all principalities and powers, and might, and "dominion, and every name that is named, not "only in this world, but in that which is to "come: and has put all things under his feet, "and has given him to be head over all things "to the church, which is his body, the fulneſs "of him who filleth all in all." Ch. i. 21, 22, 23. compare this with *Coloſ.* ii. 9, 10. "In him "dwelleth all the fulneſs of the Godhead *bodily*, "(i. e. as the church is his body.) and ye are "complete in him who is the head of all prin-"cipality and power." The great God is farther ſaid to be, "in the diſpenſation of the fulneſs of "times, gathering together in one, all things in "Chriſt,

" Chriſt, both which are in the heaven, and on " the earth, even in him." Eph. i. 10.

Jeſus Chriſt is alſo ſaid to be the *beginning, the firſt-born from the dead.*

The Greek word (αρχη) rendered, *beginning*, properly imports, a firſt authority; for we find it tranſlated, *Rule*, 1 Cor. xv. 12. and *Magiſtrate*, Luke xii. 11. and *Principality*, Tit. iii. 1. we may therefore, I apprehend, very juſtly underſtand it here, of the firſt or chief potentate in God's creation.—And then *the firſt-born from the dead*, ſhould ſeem to denote, a ſingularity of idea; none other in any age ever riſing from the dead in a public character. Or, as Lord both of the dead and of the living! the ſure pledge and earneſt of the reſurrection of all his faithful followers. And for which reaſon he ſtiles himſelf, *the reſurrection and the life!* and affirms, " that all who believe in him ſhall never die, i. e. " death ſhall have no power over them; or, " though they die, yet ſhall they live; for becauſe " he liveth, they ſhall live alſo." This determines him to be the chief potentate, as he is the firſt-born from the dead, and has aboliſhed, or made void the dominion of death.

In theſe great reſpects it is, *that in all things he might have the pre-eminence.*—Which muſt be the caſe with him, " who is the brightneſs of the Fa- " ther's glory, and the expreſs character of his " perſon." Nor can any one call in queſtion the propriety of theſe high deſcriptions given of him, if he can credit an apoſtle who has ſaid ſo expreſsly,

presſly, *that it has pleaſed the Father that in him ſhould all fulneſs dwell.**

We plainly perceive, that St. *Paul* here has his eye upon the Gentile Converts, who had their *Pantheon*, and had been accuſtomed to the idolatrous worſhip of *many Gods:* to each of which they were wont to aſcribe diſtinct powers, provinces, and ſundry divine influences; they had alſo a great variety of *demons* and *Lords*, to whom they paid homage: they even fancied, that their Gods had different ſenſitive taſtes and reliſhes. So that ſome were pleaſed with human ſacrifices; others, with thoſe of beaſts of various kinds; others, with herbs only, and the fruits of the earth.

To diſſipate and remove this thick palpable darkneſs, to correct and cure theſe groſs and debaſing ideas of the object of worſhip, it pleaſed the Father to conſtitute the man Chriſt Jeſus, the *Shechinah* of his Almighty power, the miniſter of his rule and providence; and to put all things under his feet: But then, this was not done, till after he had revealed all his truth and grace by him. So that now the chriſtian has the whole of that good, he can either hope for or reaſonably deſire, ſecured to him everlaſtingly in the apprehended great appointments of his exalted head and Lord.

The adorable Father communicates all his favours and bleſſings through this intelligible *me-*

* N. B. Though the words, *the Father*, are not in the text, but as a ſupply, yet it muſt be a proper one.

dium;

dium, whether they relate to the preſent, or to the future life of man. And what can be more reaſonable, or more worthy of God, when the terms of his favour are ſo divinely made known, and authenticated to mankind? well might St. *John* ſay, "the word was made fleſh, i. e. was "*ſhechinized* in fleſh, and dwelt among us, full "of grace and truth; and of his fulneſs we all "receive even grace after grace." He being thus qualified for all the purpoſes of his exalted appointments, we may reſt fully ſatisfied with, and truly thankful for, our having "ſuch an high "prieſt in the heavens, who is able to ſave to the "uttermoſt all who come unto God by him; ſee-"ing he ever lives the *medium* of our acceſs unto "and intercourſe with the one God the Father; "whoſe is the kingdom, the power, and the glory "for ever!"

In the above ſenſe this moſt ſublime deſcription given of the man Chriſt Jeſus, exalted to the right hand of power! has been underſtood.—

The advantageous inſtructions which mankind might receive, from the New Teſtament doctrine of our Lord's exaltation, are many. I will give a ſpecimen of ſome of thoſe beneficial teachings, in the following articles; which will be enough, I truſt, to evince *the ingratitude which there is in infidelity*.

I. From the doctrinal view we have taken, it appears evident, that no rational and juſt ideas can be formed of this account of our Lord's exaltation, unleſs we conſider it as having immediately to do with the Goſpel kingdom; i. e.

with that *new creation* which St. Paul has in his eye in this description; for so he is wont to speak of the converted Gentiles, as men delivered from darkness, by Gospel address; and brought into God's marvellous light! as children of light and of the day; in contrast to the unbelievers remaining in darkness. Nor is there any other idea to be formed of that *creating*, here applied to the man Christ Jesus; for though some would urge St. *John's* beginning his Gospel with the *word* or *logos*, and saying that all things were created by him; he does not mean, any other than the omnipotent creative word or will of God. The which word cannot constitute the person of Christ, though the same word of God did dwell with him. Or, as that Evangelist says, by its dwelling with him, it was what gave him the *glory* of being the only begotten of the Father, full of "grace and truth." That Evangelical historian, I apprehend, makes no mention of Jesus Christ, till he has finished the *preface* to his Gospel, which he does at v. 14.

Besides, as to our Lord's *creating*, it can never mean, that he brought any *new* creature into being: or, that he had any hand in the first creation; for this good reason, *viz.* because he never once says that he had: Whereas, had he been the instrument by whom God created the heaven and the earth, he must have with-held from the people, to whom he was sent to deliver the Gospel-message, a most powerful argument for their reverence of him, as their creator.

Moreover, it is impossible either that there could be more than one creator, or, that the one

one Creator could employ any inſtrument in bringing into exiſtence that which was not. *God creates without any inſtrument*;* becauſe in ſuch an act of omnipotence there could be no *medium* ſuppoſeable between cauſe and effect. And of this we are informed, by the account given of God's creating power; he ſpake, "and it was "done; he ſaid, let there be light, and there "was light: he commanded, and it ſtood faſt." Neither is there a ſingle inſtance upon record of our Lord's ever bringing any *new* ſpecies of matter into exiſtence; re-productions indeed there were many: but proper creation is only to be aſcribed to the infinite ſpirit, the firſt unoriginated and uncauſed cauſe of all!—

I will add, that our apoſtle appears, to me, to lay the greateſt *emphaſis* upon the change made in the ſpirits and morals of men by the Goſpel, as if it were a *new-creation:* for he compares it to the firſt creation; and ſays, if any man be in Chriſt, he is a *new* creature: old things are paſſed away; behold all things are become *new.* Alſo he ſpeaks, of our putting on the *new* man; and all this with great propriety, for our Lord calls it, a *new birth:* and ſays, *except a man be born again, he cannot ſee the kingdom of God.*

II. All thoſe things in heaven and earth, over which he was placed, had a *prior* exiſtence to his having the rule over them: or they had a being antecedent to his high appointments. Conſequently, for any one to ſuppoſe him, to have

* See the Creed of the Orthodox Mahometans, in Oakley's Hiſtory of the Saracens, Vol. II. p. 52.

been the *creator* of all these things, and then to imagine his being exalted or raised above them; would imply a very flagrant gross absurdity. In truth, we are not able to form any just idea of his exaltation, if it was not subsequent to his death and resurrection. It most certainly was *in futuro*, and was *the joy set before him*; by virtue of which he endured the cross, and despised the shame; and to which he has an eye when he tells his disciples, "that they shall see the heaven "open, and the Angels of God, ascending and "descending upon the son of man." And when he, in the face of the Sanhedrin, as their prisoner, said, "hereafter ye shall see the son of man "sit on the right hand of power;" and *again*, "the son of man, says he, shall come in his "glory, and all the holy Angels with him."—His exaltation must therefore have been *subsequent* to his public ministrations here on earth. And I freely own, it does not appear to me that the blessed Jesus had any real existence before he was conceived in the womb of the Virgin; when "in "the fulness of time he was made of a woman, "made under the law."—He had verily in the divine purpose, and in prophecy, a place *before* the birth of Abraham; or even before the formation of Adam: for he had a glory designed him before the foundation of the world. But then, this was in no other sense, than as he was *a Lamb slain* from the foundation of the world. And, it seems probable that our apostle, looks upon "this "revelation of the mystery, which was kept secret "since the world began, but is now made manifest, and by the scriptures of the prophets according to the commandment of the everlasting "God, made known to all nations for the obe-

"dience

" dience of faith ;" to be ſuch, that becauſe of the aſtoniſhing and adorable wiſdom of the plan, he aſcribes *to God* ONLY WISE *glory through Jesus Chriſt for ever.* *Amen.*

Theſe ideas will be very conſiſtent with that of our Lord's exaltation; whereas, the *pre-exiſtent* hypotheſis, and the notion of the world's being made by him, will not at all accord with his humiliation and exaltation: will not agree to his proper humanity: nor allow him to be an *example* of our imitation, as a partaker of fleſh and blood. But when we view him as the ſeed of the woman, and promiſed to Abraham as his deſcendant, and to be of the family of *David*, we can claim the relation to him of *brethren:* and refreſh ourſelves with the honours which the Father has conferred upon him as our vital head, and as Lord both of the dead and of the living: ten thouſand benefits we derive from the adorable plan of the Goſpel-Inſtitution.*

III. The exaltation of Jeſus Chriſt, all his high appointments are the gracious and Fatherly-beſtowments of the infinite Spirit; whoſe inceſſant preſence with him, is what furniſheth his capacity of exerciſing thoſe high offices to which he has been exalted.—We have full evidence of this; ſince it was to the *end* of God's making himſelf ſo gloriouſly known in his paternal regards to mankind, that the Goſpel-plan was ori-

* If any one would ſee the argument, in its full force, let him conſult *the Letter written in the year* 1730.—Alſo *the true doctrine of the New Teſtament concerning Jeſus Chriſt conſidered;* which deny the pre-exiſtence of Chriſt.

ginally laid, and to which end all preparatory meaſures have been taken from the beginning.— "*Father*, ſays Jeſus, *glorify thy name. Again*, "now is God *glorified* in the ſon of man."— St. Paul, to the ſame purpoſe, ſays, "every "tongue ſhall confeſs him Lord to the praiſe and "*glory* of God the Father,—and he tells us, that "the adoption of us as *Sons*, is to the praiſe and "*glory* of his grace!"

And yet, becauſe of thoſe ſuperior honours which the Father has been pleaſed to confer on the man Chriſt Jeſus, many have aſcribed to this our bleſſed Lord an uncreated, underived divine nature; and to repreſent him as "God equal "with the *Father!*" nay, there are not a *few* who pay him the homage which is due only to the one God: but then, theſe have imagined, that the infinite ſpirit can be divided, and ſplit into "three parts or perſons, the ſame in ſubſtance, "as well as equal in power and glory:" which when duly conſidered, will be ſeen to be the quinteſſence of a prophane and enormous abſurdity; or, the moſt debaſing, depraved idea of the one object of ſupreme homage.

They therefore muſt have their eyes faſt ſealed, who can be ſo ſtupid as to ſuppoſe, that an eternal being of infinite wiſdom, almighty power, and an immenſity of preſence can be either *abaſed*, or *exalted*; that God can be both ſovereign and ſubject: or, be paſſively obedient unto, and then reward himſelf.—*Again*, what extravagance would there be in ſuppoſing the unbeginning, unchangable, everlaſting God, to be the *firſt-born* of every creature, and the *image* of himſelf! to be the

firſt-

firſt-born from the dead! the beginning or the *chief* of his own creation! And all this, when on the contrary, theſe epithets are the moſt expreſsly deſcriptive characteriſtics of a created being; or, of one individual of that ſame ſpecies of creatures, whereof he is ſaid to be the *firſt-born*; i. e. over whom God has given him ſuch pre-eminence. So that the *all things*, ſaid to be created *by* him and *for* him muſt only denote God's orderance, diſpoſal, guidance and government of them by his inſtrumentality. No other ſhould here ſeem to be the natural ſenſe of the word, *create*, as, I truſt, has been ſufficiently ſhewn.

And in confirmation of this ſenſe, God's *not giving the Spirit by meaſure* to the man Chriſt Jeſus; during his earthly miniſtrations, was needful to the purpoſe of preparing mankind for giving due credit to his high and heavenly appointments.—The whole ſcenery of his public-life, was accordingly an earneſt to himſelf, as well as to the world, that the great God deſigned to make him the inſtrument of his power and goodneſs, in the Government and Providence which he exerciſeth both in heaven and earth. But the being who has theſe honours conferred upon him, can be no other than a *creature*, who muſt owe thoſe very divine honours to the one ſupreme God and Father of all!—*Again*,

To ſuppoſe the *receiver* of the recompence of reward, to be equal to the *giver* of that recompence, can be no other than an aſtoniſhing extravagance! or, to aſcribe to him the *receiver* incommunicable perfections, is to give the glory due only to God, to a man, who is but the *recipient*; God having exalted him to the right hand of power.

At the ſame time, we chearfully own, the bleſſed Jeſus, whom we view as thus exalted, claims an honourable regard due to God's repreſentative; the prime miniſter in his church and kingdom; but not as the original infinite ſource of ſuch delegated authority and power.—

This ſame St. Paul, has given us the cleareſt and moſt determinate ideas of the *ſubordination* of the exalted Jeſus to his God and Father—when he ſays to the Corinthians, "I would have you "know, that the head of every man, is Chriſt; "that the head of the woman, is the man; and "that the head of Chriſt, is God." No ſcale of ideas can be more expreſſive and inſtructive, than this of the ſeveral claſſes of ſuperiority and ſubordinacy which are in the eſtabliſhed plan of God's rule and government.

It was a good obſervation made by a learned pen, upon Heb. iv. 9. that the character of *ſitting on the throne*, belongs only to God the Father.*

IV. The diſtinguiſhed honours conferred on the man Chriſt Jeſus, had for their obvious *reaſon* and *ground*, his diſtinguiſhed, his matchleſs piety and obedience. Nor can any view of his exaltation be more ſatisfactory and refreſhing to an human

* ὁ καθημενος επι του θρονου never belongs to Chriſt in St. John's ſtyle. See an anonymous pamphlet, entitled, *the Apoſtles Creed better than the Aſſemblies Catechiſm*, p. 61. Printed 1720, ſaid to be by Mr. Joſeph Hallet junior.

mind;

mind; as it gives the moſt adorable ideas of Almighty God, contemplated as a moral Governor. —We ſee in it his *love of righteouſneſs*, and his fatherly concern to inſpire mankind with a firſt ſolicitude to pleaſe him, by doing all his will:— and hence it is, that the Chriſtian is exhorted to look to Jeſus as the author, the leader-on, and the finiſher of his faith;—and as the captain of his ſalvation, who was perfected through ſufferings:—God thus placeth before the eye of man, the fixed, eternal connexions which there are between a love of truth, and ſupreme happineſs.—It thus renders the vaſt deſigns of heaven familiar to us: and we can read the tranſporting lines of his truth and grace, in their inſeparable and everlaſting eſtabliſhment.—

No *Sceptic*, no *Infidel* can point out ſo much as the ſhadow of human contrivance in any part of the Goſpel plan; nor can he produce one mark of defect in the evidence of our Lord's exaltation; or ſhew it to be unworthy of our higheſt gratitude and praiſe! for it holds up to open view, the infinite importance of our doing the will of God, from the reward conferred on the perſonal obedience of Jeſus Chriſt; and leaves no room for the leaſt excuſe, or apology for our diſobedience, in any given circumſtance of human trial; and it alſo thus indulges, with the utmoſt ſcope of exertion, the moſt refined, ſublime, and boundleſs wiſh, deſire, and delight of the ſoul of man.—Hence we may be bold to ſay, it appears to us, that the great and good God could not have more *glorified* himſelf; or have appeared more adorable to the human race, than in this laſt diſpenſation of his truth and grace by the man Jeſus

Chriſt our Lord. So that there muſt be *ingratitude in infidelity*.

V. All ſcruples in the Chriſtian about making his addreſſes in the name, or through the mediation of the exalted Jeſus, do inſtantly die away, when once contemplated by him as that SHECHINAH of God, by whoſe inſtrumentality he is directing, protecting, and governing his church and world.—We are likewiſe, by this contemplation, much more able to form an idea of *locality* in the preſence of the beatifying glory! i. e. we can better conceive of the bliſsful heavenly abodes, by a circumſcribed, viſible, converſible perſonage of our own ſpecies, placed at the right hand of power; the moſt glorious manifeſtations of an inviſible incomprehenſible ſpirit, are, by this *medium* made more fatherly, familiar, and felicitating!

However, to the Infidel, the *mediation* of Jeſus, as ſyſtematically or generally underſtood, has been, and yet is a great ſtumbling-block. Whereas, would he but fix his eye upon the New Teſtament, that divine and rational repreſentation of this *medium* of acceſs and addreſs; he would be perſuaded, that this is the moſt informing, divinely pleaſing, and delightful plan that could be laid for the direction of our homage; foraſmuch as ſince "it has pleaſed the Father, *that in him* "*ſhould all fulneſs dwell*," we are naturally led to reverence him as the great *medium*, or miniſter of all divine communications of grace and mercy. We addreſs the one God, through the mediation of this one Lord, whom he has made head over all things to his church, the FULNESS *of him who filleth all in all!* But yet, in this direction of our homage, we consider the man Christ Jesus, as no other than the MEDIUM; and not as that being, between whom and us he mediates. And how clearly does this correspond with the natural ideas of man, who ever sought a *medium* of worship?—

It is astonishing that any should pretend to make use of the name of Jesus as a mediator; and all the while worship him as if he was *no mediator*; but ultimately as the one supreme! On the contrary, the rational Christian distinguishes in the object of his worship, between the Father and the Son—between the *sovereign* and the *subject*,* or minister of his rule and government. He knows, that that fulness of the Godhead which dwells bodily, or so communicatively in Jesus Christ, is not that Jesus Christ himself, with whom, or in whom such a fulness dwells.—and thus the purity of Christian worship is preserved, and appears to be rational, and becoming the most perfect manifestations of divine truth and mercy.—

VI. Our blessed Lord's being exalted above all order of beings, invisible as well as visible, will relieve the human mind from any manner of uneasy or painful apprehensions about *apparitions*, *evil-spirits*, or *demons*.—

Under former dispensations, the great God did make use of the visible ministration of Angels; and by their hands did both preserve and punish

* 1 Cor. xv. 27, 28.

man-

mankind. The Sacred Scriptures do plainly teach this doctrine; but inasmuch as under the Gospel-dispensation, all created powers, visible and invisible, are put in subjection to the sceptre of Jesus, we have no reason to apprehend any kind of injury or harm from evil angels, or demons.— The *Jews*, we know, were wont to ascribe all incurable distempers and calamities to their causality.

And much noise has been made in the world about apparitions and prodigies preter-natural. Even in the darker ages of a corrupted Christian profession, men have not come behind either *Jews* or *Pagans* in various inventions to fill vulgar minds with fearful images. And a very learned writer on prodigies, says, "*Rome Pagan* was as "good at inventing stories of prodigies and appa-"ritions of the Gods, as *Rome Christian* of mira-"cles and apparitions of Saints."*

It is no small satisfaction to the Christian, that his Lord has a name given him above every name: and that all must bow to him, whether things in heaven, in earth, or under the earth. This consideration sets the christian *free* from all dread of apparitions, or of evil spirits; and will not suffer him to be disturbed by fanciful ideas of their mal-influence. For notwithstanding there has been no visible assistance afforded from good Angels, since the Apostles, as there was in their age; yet we may reasonably conclude, that in every succeeding age of the church, they must

* SPENCER on prodigies, p. 8.

be

be employed in the Chriſtian's favor; foraſmuch as they are all ſent forth to miniſter to them who are, or ſhall be the heirs of ſalvation.

VII. The exaltation of the man Chriſt Jeſus, peremptorily and abſolutely forbids all *creature-worſhip*. There are ſeveral inſtances on ſacred record, where the worſhip of Saints and Angels is expreſsly condemned. St. *Paul* and *Barnabas* when they had miraculouſly healed the cripple at *Lyſtra*, forbad the idolatry; and St. *Peter* would not ſuffer any religious worſhip to be paid him by *Cornelius*, though he had conſidered that apoſtle as only a divine meſſenger.—And St. *John's* conductor through the viſionary heavenly ſcenes, reprimanded his falling down at his feet.—"*See*, "ſaid he, *thou do it not:* for I am thy fellow "ſervant, and of thy brethren the prophets, &c. "worſhip thou God."

A learned writer obſerved, that the idolatry of *Angel-worſhip* is condemned in this epiſtle, ch. ii. 18, 19. "The Jews had received the doctrine, "and the converts from among them brought "along with them what was borrowed in a great "meaſure from the heathen Philoſophers; and "*Philo* ſays,* *there are other ſouls moſt pure and* "*good, who have a greater and more divine judg*"*ment and underſtanding, and who deſire nothing at* "*all that is earthly*: *theſe are the preſidents or* "*princes of the Almighty, like the eyes and ears of* "*ſome great King, beholding, and hearing all things:* "*theſe the Philoſophers call* demons, *but the Hebrew*

* De Somnis, p. 586.

"*ſcrip-*

" *scriptures use to call them, and that most properly,* " Angels; *for they carry the Father's commandments* " *to his children, and the children to the Father:* " *and therefore the scripture represents them as ascend-* " *ing and descending. It is expedient*, says he, *for us* " *mortals to make use of such mediators.* Again, *if* " *Angels were such mrdiators, a worship was due to* " *them*, viz. *the saints should offer up their prayers* " *to God by them, offering them up to them, that they* " *might present them to God.*"

Now, my Author observes, " this mischief con- " tinued long in Phrygia and Pisidia; hence the " council, that met at Laodicea in Phrygia, made " a law against praying to Angels; and to this " very day,* says *Theodoret*, are to be seen among " them, and in the neighbouring parts, the ora- " tories of St. *Michael*; and that the *Essenes*, took " great care about the name of Angels."

I would add, that the worship of the *papal-church* is anti-christian, and idolatrous: for it makes use of many mediators. But unto us Christians, " there is but one God; and but ONE MEDIATOR " between God and man, the man Christ Jesus."

It is said, I am afraid too justly, that that shocking popish *Superstition* is now gaining ground, in a protestant Christian nation—but if it be true, it can do no other than deprave and unchristianize the spirit of our people—for the worship of papal-Rome, is not at all fit for men, considered either

* About the fourth century, So Mr. *James Pierce* on the place. See his paraphrase.

as rational beings, or as christians. And were it not for the dissipation and debauchery, which are become epidemical, and an avowed aim in public a————n, to give a despotic sway to the British Sceptre, we might well be astonished at the delusion. To *conclude*,

It is presumed, that the truth of the proposition in the Title-page has been made evident, *viz.* "that the ingratitude of infidelity is proveable, "from the humiliation and exaltation of Jesus "Christ being the most beneficial appointments "that are within the known plan of God's moral "government;" for that whoever ruminates upon the seven views above taken of the advantageous instruction which mankind may receive from those appointments, must have the highest reverence of the New Testament writings, as an *inestimable treasure!* which informs us, that he is of God made unto us wisdom, and righteousness, and sanctification, and redemption; for by the whole of Gospel address, we are led to glory in it, as the wisdom of God, and the power of God; inasmuch as Jesus Christ was raised from the dead, and glory given him, that our *faith* and *hope* might be in God.

FINIS.

ERRATA.

Page 4. l. 22. for Ψυκη read Ψυχη.
5. l. 5. from bottom, for *lie,* read *lye.*
25, Note, dele *and.*
26. l. 3. from bottom, for *as* read *which.*

www.ingramcontent.com/pod-product-compliance
Lightning Source LLC
Chambersburg PA
CBHW022037080426
42733CB00007B/863

9783337148508